MW01707956

Steamship Cayuga

Toronto's Ship of Romance

Carole M. Lidgold

Published 1996 by
Brookridge Publishing House
Scarborough, Ontario

Canadian Cataloguing in Publication Data

Lidgold, Carole M.
Steamship Cayuga

Includes Bibliographical references

1. Cayuga (Steamer) - History I. Title

VM627.05L52 1996 387.2'436
C96-931430-2

ISBN # 0-9698244-3-2

Cover Photograph Submitted by: John M. Ferguson

Edited by: Jim Harris

Printed and bound in Canada by: AIIM Group
Aurora, Ontario

Dedication

To my husband Gord, and our daughter Lori, who never knew Cayuga

Acknowledgements

Special thanks to Jim Smith, of Niagara-on-the-Lake, for all his help in acquiring research documents and photographs.

Many thanks to Tim Sequin, Richard Gerrard, and Lisa, of the Toronto Historical Society for their help in research.

To Irene van Bavel, National Archives of Canada, thanks for your help in locating the photos of Cayuga and the speedy delivery of these photos.

The photo archives of The Globe & Mail was extremely helpful in locating the photographs, as well as the article about them. Thank you very much for your help.

It's a very small world when the daughter of Cpt. J.D. Strachan lives down the road. Thanks to Isobel Cooney for the conversation and photos of her father.

Special thanks to Betty (Cooper) Gordon for allowing me to share her story.

And lastly to Jim Harris, of the Canadian Authors Association, thanks for reviewing and editing my manuscript.

Betty Cooper on Cayuga 1944

Don Gordon - R.C.A.F. - on Cayuga August 1944

Cayuga changed my life. In July 1943 The Canada Life Assoc. Co., where I worked, hosted a midnight cruise for the airmen stationed in town, for which they received free tickets, which also included free refreshments. He was hungry, broke and lacking anything better to do, strolled over from Exhibition Park barracks to check it out. I was there with my friend because my boy friend was caught two-timing me. I wanted to show him I could find a tall, dark, handsome airman from the west.

They lined up the girls on one side of the dock and guys on the other. Because I was a redhead this young man chose me and on the boat we went. He couldn't dance (we blamed it on the rough water). We didn't eat because it was a meatless day, but he was polite, interested and all of the above. It was too good an opportunity to pass up when he asked for my phone number. Thirteen months later we were married and sailed on the Cayuga to Niagara Falls for our one week honeymoon.

Returning to Queenston by bus for the trip home we found to our dismay that the boat had left without us, already filled to capacity. We spent most of the lovely warm night in each other's arms, sitting on the luggage carts on the dock at Queenston awaiting its return. Arriving home at 6:00 a.m. in North Toronto, I got heck from my Dad, whom I was still living with as my husband was now stationed in Manitoba.

When the war was over and he returned to me, we moved to Nobel on Georgian Bay to raise our family; then to U.S. as victims of the Arrow cancellation, for six years. Then we moved back to Canada, (Pembroke), and by the time we returned to the Toronto area, Cayuga was gone, so we never sailed on her again.

My older brothers have fond memories of our family trips as young children to Niagara Falls on Cayuga and the exciting ride on the open-sided trolley along the gorge. My Dad even bought property on Lundy's Lane and the locals grew potatoes on it. As times got tighter he sold it - can you imagine the value now?

Before the war my eldest brother was stationed at Niagara-on-the-Lake in the permanent Army and the firing range area is still there. Many, many years later he returned to that area, living on Queenston Rd. a block or so from where the docks used to be, across the river from Lewiston and the Riverside Restaurant. He knows all the history of the War of 1812 and Isaac Brock's resting place. He used to give us a guided tour whenever we visited him. His daughter and family now live in a subdivision near where he trained before the war. (He was one of the first soldiers to be shipped overseas and brought back a beautiful war bride in 1945, now deceased). Now he is getting on, his health is poor and he lives in the senior's apartment on that same property. Imagine his memories! What a coincidence!

My other brother lives in Scarborough and also has fond memories of Cayuga, Ontario's Love Boat.

Betty (Cooper) Gordon
Bramalea, Ontario

CONTENTS

Steamship Cayuga

Cayuga 1906 - National Archives of Canada
C26022

The Beginning!

Superintendent Angstrom shouted "Let go!"

Miss Mary Oster clutched the bottle of wine tied by a ribbon to the bow of the ship, swung it toward the hull and cried "Good luck" as the bottle smashed against steel.

A crowd gathered at the foot of Bathurst St. in Toronto, Ontario. Heavy rain fell and a strong east wind buffeted against them. In spite of the weather they stayed to watch as the 317' ship slid gently into the cold water of Lake Ontario. The date was March 3, 1906.

Roy Snider, a reporter for the Telegram remarks on the launching:

> *"...it was on a dull day in the early spring of 1907, that they side launched her just east of the foot of Bathurst St. and west of the northern elevator."*
>
> *"All the Toronto papers were*

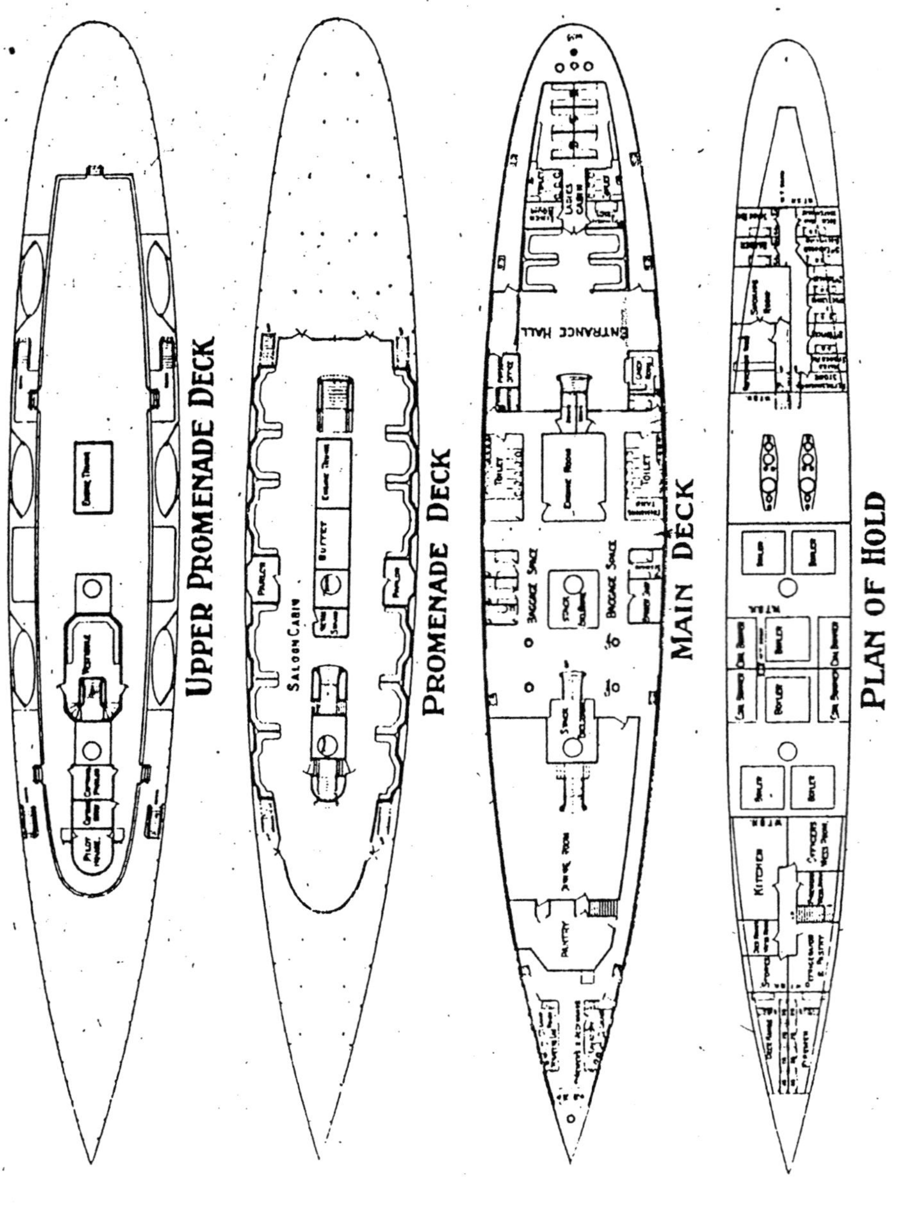

Railway and Marine World - 1905

there and photographers as there were in those days, and artists. People climbed to vantage points in the northern elevator and on top of buildings, sheds and box cars, to watch the ceremony."

After the launch, to celebrate the momentous occasion, the Directors of the companies retired to the King Edward Hotel. And this was a significant moment that would be remembered almost 90 years later. This ship was destined to sail forever in the memories of her passengers and crew, never to be forgotten for the pleasure she gave.

Designed as a seasonal day-sailer, Cayuga, as thc ship was latcr namcd, was an elegant edition to the fleet of the Niagara Navigation Company. A. Angstrom, a noted marine architect, gave Cayuga all the best features to make sailing on her an exciting, comfortable trip. She was 39' 6" wide with an overall length of 317', a depth of 18', with four levels and two smoke stacks angled toward the stern giving her an appearance of great speed. The pilot house, situated on the Upper Promenade Deck, had tall windows in a rounded, flat-topped tower. An open bridge stretched from each side of the pilot house where the actual piloting of the ship was conducted.

The lowest level held the powerful engines and boilers. Cayuga had two vertical inverted, direct-acting, quadruple steam engines. Seven coal-fired marine boilers, 11' x 12', were fitted with two corrugated furnaces and a system of heated draughts. The steam pressure was 210 lbs. and Cayuga's top speed was 22 ½ M.P.H. (miles per hour). Driven by twin screws, Cayuga was able to maneuver easier leaving and entering port.

The steel hull was designed in such a way as to make her almost unsinkable. At least there were no icebergs in Lake Ontario to test this theory. Seven bulkheads made eight water-tight compartments. Bilge keels were included in the hull to reduce the rolling motion. Also in the lower level, or Orlop Deck, was the kitchen situated at the bow end. In the stern was a smoking room and crew quarters.

To enter Cayuga three gangways led into the main deck. The forward one was for passengers and express shipments.

Passengers and baggage entered through the middle gangway. For passengers without baggage, they used the aft gangway.

When entering the aft gangway passengers were in the entrance hall. The ceiling was made of heavy beams. On this level, near the bow, was the mahogany dining room where delicious meals were served by white-coated waiters. At the stern was the ladies' cabin. To get to the next level, the Promenade Deck, passengers used the 7' wide stairway. This was a magnificent staircase made of Cathedral Oak. At the top of the stairway, at each side, there was a doorway allowing access to the open deck, or entrance to the Saloon cabin.

The Saloon cabin was a gracious place to watch the passing scenery. Eight bow windows on each side allowed a grand view as well as a place for small groups to gather - especially couples who wanted a private place to share romantic moments. Hearty passengers, who enjoyed the sunshine and stiff breezes, sank into chairs lined along the deck. At the bow of Cayuga the upper deck formed a ceiling and gave a bit of protection from rainy weather. At the stern there was

Submitted by Jim Smith from Don Van Alstine

also a ceiling where life preservers were stored. Bands played here, on weekend moonlight cruises, and passengers tried to dancc on thc swaying dcck.

Sea gulls squealed and sailed on the breeze behind Cayuga. Passengers encouraged them by tossing bits of bread from their lunches. The sea gulls were constant companions following Cayuga on her voyage across Lake Ontario.

From the Saloon cabin a stairway led to the Upper Promenade Deck. Or from the outside deck passengers could climb the narrow, open stairway to the next level. These were located outside the Saloon cabin at both the bow and the stern. Here the breeze was strong and sometimes smoke from the funnels left bits of coal dust on the passengers' clothing.

On this level was located the 'monkey's island'. Overlooking the ship was the pilot house and bridge. At the base was a raised area for passengers to sit on deck chairs. Lifeboats were securely fastened on the outside of the railing, below the monkey's island, covered with tarpaulins to keep them dry for emergency use.

Cayuga's trial run by the builder Canadian Ship Building Co. was held on July 27, 1907. Everyone, owners and builders, wcrc vcry plcascd with thc ship. In mid August of 1907 Cayuga was given speed trials. Ninety-four miles from Toronto to Charlotte and back. Cayuga's average speed was 21½ M.P.H. A second test of 30 miles, which is the distance between Toronto and Niagara, was held and Cayuga had a speed of 22½ M.P.H. However her first recorded run was held on June 10, 1907.

The cost to build Cayuga was reduced because of late completion and delivery. Cayuga cost $ 266,137.90 to build and was able to carry 2500 passengers per trip.

While owned by The Niagara Navigation Co. her smoke stacks were painted crimson with black bands. The hull was painted black, up to the main deck rail, and the rest painted white.

Although a beautiful ship, Cayuga was very long - too long for dry-docking in Toronto. Kingston, Ontario, was the only place Cayuga could go for repairs. In 1907 the first repair was for longer propeller blades.

So it began, a pleasure cruise across

Lake Ontario through two wars and into the cherished memories of so many passengers and crew. I was fortunate to have been a passscngcr on Cayuga for approximatcly 12 years, at the end of that era of romantic cruises on Lake Ontario.

Submitted by Jim Smith from Don Van Alstine

Naming the Ship

The Niagara Navigation Company held a contest to name their newest ship. There was a stipulation that the name was to begin with "C" and end with "A". This was in keeping with the names of their other ships - Chicora, Chippewa, Corona and Cibola.

The contest was advertised in newspapers and the prize was "Book Tickets". A total of 233 names were suggested. From these suggestions the name 'Cayuga' was chosen. The spelling of the name was selected in recognition of the Indian tribes on the south shore of Lake Ontario in the area where the ship would sail, and also because of Lake Cayuga in New York state. Rejected spellings of the name were "Kukey", "Cugga", "Kiucky", "Cyuga" and "Kiugeagch". Also, in Ontario near the shores of Lake Ontario, is the town of Cayuga.

Cayuga on the route between Toronto and Queenston Heights
National Archives of Canada - PA49824 - Dept. Of the Interior

The Route

Cayuga docked at Pier 9 at the Port of Toronto (Bay St. and Yonge St.) and in the heat of summer offered an easy escape to city dwellers. In Cayuga's early sailing days workers had a half-day holiday on Saturday and crowded onto the ship. Passengers sailed safely through the Eastern Gap into the wide waters of Lake Ontario. From here Cayuga steered across to Niagara-on-the-Lake in approximately two hours.

As Cayuga enters the Niagara River on one side is Fort Niagara, high on a rocky cliff in the United States. On the other side is the beach where swimmers wave their hands, at passengers lining the railings, while they dive in and out of the rolling waves Cayuga creates. A loud whistle booms out the announcement that the ship is arriving at the dock. Passengers line up on the roofed, wooden dock eager to board for the short sail to Queenston Heights. Other passengers disembark to spend a few hours in the town or for a longer stay. Whistling again, Cayuga moves away from the dock and maneuvers into the strong current of the river. This part of the journey is sometimes treacherous.

Queenston Heights is the last stop on the Niagara River. Beyond this point are the rapids fed by the pouring waters of Niagara Falls. The current is very strong and navigation is tricky. Cayuga was built for easy navigation with her twin screws.

High above the docks is Queenston Heights Park where many travelers go for picnics. Most often they had to climb the many, many steps leading from the road above the dock to the park. It was a trek for the hardy. I remember climbing these steps with my mother and sister. Other travelers could reach the park by road, a longer distance but an easier walk.

In the early 1900s there was an open railway system that transported travelers to Niagara Falls. In later years buses were available to travel to the Falls.

On this same route, until 1939, was the Chicora and the Chippewa, a side wheel paddle boat. The Niagara Navigation

Company offered six lake crossings per day so passengers could travel on one vessel to Niagara and Queenston, then return on anothcr. Bccausc of agc both Chicora, first, then Chippewa were retired leaving Cayuga as the only passenger ship. At this time, 1939, Cayuga was owned by Canada Steamship Lines who had merged with Niagara Navigation Company in 1913.

In the early years fares were affordable for most people. In 1918 a one way fare from Toronto to Queenston Heights was $ 1.45. The return fare was $ 2.40. This was also the fare to Niagara-on-the-Lake. In 1957 the fares were still affordable. Adult return fare was $ 3.90, one way $ 2.20. Children's fare return was $ 1.95 and one way was $ 1.10.

On weekday mornings in 1955, also on Saturday and Sunday, Cayuga's first trip began at 9:00 a.m. From Wednesday to Sunday passengers could also board her at 2:55 p.m. For an evening cruise Monday, Tuesday and Thursday, passengers boarded at 6:00 p.m. Then there was the moonlight cruise where many young couples pledged their love while dancing to various bands.

Cayuga in the Eastern Gap - National Archives of Canada
PA87508 - John Boyd

Bands performed on the Promenade Deck at Cayuga's stern. Passengers danced, or tried to, on the heaving deck. Many romanccs flourishcd bcncath thc moonlight on the open deck. Cayuga left Toronto (1955) at 9:45 p.m. on Friday, Saturday and holidays. At this time of night, even in the hottest part of summer, travelling on the open deck was a cold experience.

When Cayuga used coal she docked at Lewiston, U.S.A. to load up for the journey home. Passenger fare from Queenston to Lewiston, in 1918, was ten cents.

Cayuga stopped to refuel at Lewiston during the supper hour. Built into the side of the Escarpment the coal silo was filled with Pennsylvannia steamer coal. Two-wheeled carts, filled at the bottom of the silo, were pushed over a metal gang plank into the ship's coal bunkers with steel, man-hole shaped covers. The coal silo, today, is still at Lewiston. However, in 1938 a tremendous build up of ice destroyed the Lewiston dock as well as the Queenston dock. The Lewiston dock was never rebuilt, the Queenston dock was rebuilt, and Cayuga no longer stopped at Lewiston.

Cayuga in Dry Dock 1918 - National Archives of Canada
PA136344 - Andrew Merrilees

MECHANICAL FAULTS AND OTHER PROBLEMS

Cayuga looked mechanically healthy from the outside but inside there were problems. In November 1924 an inspection of her seven boilers revealed corrosion and 'wasting'. A re-inspection in January 1925 revealed extensive leakage. Cayuga needed immediate repairs or the pressure of her boilers would have to be reduced. Repairs were made but during the next twenty years more problems were encountered with her boilers.

Government regulations demanded changes. If the hull portholes were less than 24" above the water line when Cayuga was loaded, deadlights must be added. In the crew accommodations some portholes had been left open and water had entered the rooms. Inclement weather or waves from passing vessels had pushed the water through the

Submitted by Jim Smith from Don Van Alstine

open portholes.

Repairs could only be made on Cayuga at the busy Kingston, Ontario docks. This was due to Cayuga's length. In 1929 Cayuga was fitted with a new starboard tail shaft and propeller. Then in 1933 inspectors discovered new faults in her deteriorating boilers. September 1934 Cayuga had various repairs done to her sheerstrakes. Five years later, May 1939, the port screw (propeller) was refitted. These repairs did not solve the problem.

The following year, May 1940, more repairs were completed. An entire new port tailshaft was attached complete with a cast steel hub. Then over-crowding of passengers brought more necessary changes as well as more boiler problems.

Two more lifeboats were added to Cayuga for safety of passengers in case of emergency. Then a further inspection of the seven boilers revealed major problems. The boilers, once round, were deformed out of shape from the constant steam pressure. However, Cayuga was deemed sailable for another season with her boilers as they were.

Once again, May 1942, Cayuga's

tailshafts were repaired. One new blade was fitted on the port screw. The next month, June 1942, inspectors ordered further changcs.

There were too many passengers and not enough seating. To alleviate this problem the men's toilets on the main deck were relocated to space once occupied by the officers' cabins near the engine casing. Extra deck patrols were added to keep passageways clear. In the general saloon the stairway from the cargo deck was closed except while Cayuga was in dock. Stairways to the pilot house and upper bridge were removed while the ladder to the pilot house was extended. Officers could now reach the upper bridge without passing through the passenger deck.

On the Orlop deck in the crew quarters a major problem was rectified. There was poor ventilation, requiring the addition of air-conditioning fans. As well, the boilers were still in very poor condition. In 1945 inspectors ordered that something be done with the boilers.

Inspectors in 1946 reduced passenger capacity to 1850 and 75 crew members. Also noted was the incorrect positioning of the lifeboats on the upper promenade deck which may cause delays in an emergency. This was the reason Cayuga had to carry fewer passengers. Finally her boilers were replaced.

Instead of burning coal Cayuga's two new watertube boilers burned oil. To replace the weight lost by removing the five boilers, 75 long tons of permanent iron ballast was placed in the bottom of Cayuga. The main steam pipes were replaced to carry the new fuel. Cayuga also required new pumps to keep a working pressure of 210 p.s.i. This ensured a continuation of a good sailing speed. This was not the end of repairs.

Removing the old boilers from Cayuga presented a problem. A large opening was cut in Cayuga and the first two boilers removed with no difficulty. Cayuga became unstable when efforts were made to remove the third boiler. The boilers were cut up, then lifted out as the new equipment was moved aboard.

Canada Steamship Lines wanted to remove the second, unnecessary funnel. This would ruin the "lines" of Cayuga and the company was persuaded to leave both funnels in place. One funnel was working while the other was there for "looks".

City of Toronto Archives - SC231-966A

The ballast was steel rails placed between the frames and floor in the engine room and aft boiler room bilges. These were cut and placcd in groups. This produccd a weight concentration in an area that hadn't been there before. This may have been the reason that caused the lightly built hull to twist with stress when the engine was running at full power.

Cayuga was drydocked in Kingston in August 1948. The first length of Cayuga's starboard propeller had broken with a loss of the tailshaft and propeller. The car ferry Ontario No. I gave her its spare tailshaft which was modified to fit. A spare screw was also fitted on Cayuga. In September 1948 Cayuga struck bottom travelling through the Eastern Gap of Toronto Harbour. Inspection at Kingston showed there was no damage.

More problems occurred in October 1949. Cayuga had two new solid manganese, bronze screws fitted. At this time small fractures were discovered in the intermediate shafts in the keyway. New shafts were fitted as well as a renewed port tailshaft. The burning of the Noronic at the Toronto dock caused further additions.

Fire detection equipment must be installed. Cayuga's owners Canada Steamship Lines complied with the safety regulations in 1950. Fire hydrants, 2" in diameter were installed in 53 locations. In the boiler room and condenser room, steam smothering equipment was added. In all decks automatic fire sprinklers were installed. Fire-resistant bulkheads were fitted as well as an alarm system. Portable fire extinguishers were located at fire-vulnerable areas. With these improvements Cayuga was allowed to continue carrying 1850 passengers.

Damage resulted as Cayuga left the Niagara-on-the-Lake dock in July 1951. She struck a submerged object in the river and damaged the starboard propeller. The shaft was re-aligned and in September Cayuga was fitted with a new propeller. Back in Toronto, after all these repairs and additions, Cayuga was taken out of service due to lack of passenger traffic.

New owners took over but problems lay ahead. At the end of the first season Cayuga suffered extensive damage when she hit the pilings at Queenston. Twenty-nine sponson braces on the port side were fractured or buckled. These were replaced during the winter layup. The Department of Transportation then demanded changes to some of the fire system.

The steam smothering system in the boiler room was not satisfactory. Controls had to be added outside the boiler room to stop the fans and close the dampers. Closable plates must be fitted over the spaces around the funnels where they passed through the deck, an impossible task. A foam system must be added that would quickly fill the boiler room to the top. Otherwise a carbon dioxide system would have to be installed that would produce 25% saturation. The new owners couldn't afford these expensive additions. Another Government concern was the galley stove.

This stove still used coal as a fuel. It had to be converted to oil. The first fuel tank, because of the thickness of the steel, was condemned and replaced with a better tank. More problems were discovered in 1955.

An inspection of the machinery revealed that the first intermediate pressure crank pin was cracked. The crankshaft would have to be replaced. This was completed in early

1956. The season of 1957 brought further damage when the captain had a heart attack.

Cayuga struck her starboard side heavily against Pier Ten, the east side of Yonge St. Under the guidance of a new captain, Cayuga once again landed heavily and damaged her port side. The damage was repaired. In July a piece of wire became wound around the port propeller. Inspectors criticized other faults.

A self-contained diesel fire pump with sea suction was installed. Faults were criticized by the inspectors with the electrical systems. Inspectors also attended the fire drills when Cayuga was at the Imperial Oil dock in Toronto. The owners could no longer afford to operate Cayuga.

Tugs towed Cayuga to a berth along the north harbour wall between Bathurst St. and Spadina Ave. Winds forced Cayuga against the dock and she sustained heavy damage, as well as growing shabby from neglect. Severe damage occurred to the main deck cabin aft on the port side. There would be no more repairs and in 1961 she was dismantled by Greenspoon Bros.

THE RACE THAT WAS?

Did Cayuga race the *Turbinia* steamship in 1908? An oiler on Cayuga, a Mr. MacDonald told this version in 1936 to Don Page who was an oiler on the *Kingston*. He mentioned that Cayuga somehow strayed towards Hamilton just as *Turbinia* left the pier at Burlington for Toronto. Mr. MacDonald says that thc two boats raccd sidc by sidc for approximately an hour. *Turbinia's* steam power couldn't sustain the "flat out" volume and she had to slow down. On Cayuga her Chief Engineer opened impulse valves to the high pressure valve chests and Cayuga continued at high speed. Or is that the way it happened?

Malcolm McGrath, a close friend of Alan Howard, says his father was on Cayuga at that time. This version is that Cayuga and *Turbinia* were on a regular run and it was on the Niagara River when the race began. Neither steamship was near Hamilton.

However further investigation of this

race revealed other facts. In 1908 a report from the annual meeting of the Turbine Steamship Company (who owned Turbinia) said that thc ship would only havc two round trips per day to Hamilton and Toronto.

In his book *A Century of Sail and Steam on the Niagara River,* Barlow Cumberland states the date of this race as 1907. On May 20, 1907 the Turbine Steamship Company announced that *Turbinia* would not do the two Hamilton to Toronto trips. Instead *Turbinia* would sail in the morning from Hamilton to Toronto then make two trips to Niagara-on-the-Lake and Lewiston then back to Hamilton in the evening.

It appears that the two steamships had a competitive race but the date is uncertain. What is known is that Cayuga survived the *Turbinia* by many years.

J.R.G. Bleasy, and his wife, with the model he built now on display at the Marine Museum, Kingston, Ontario

CAYUGA TODAY

As well as memories there are physical reminders of the gracious Cayuga. The Toronto Historical Society maintains a Cayuga Room in the Stanley Barracks located in Toronto Exhibition Place. The artifacts consist of photographs of several of the captains, the Union Jack flag from Cayuga, ticket stubs, schedules, the fog horn, pressure gauge, twin wheel and stand, just to mention a few.

Several models have been built of Cayuga. The model built by J.R.G. Bleasby is on display at The Marine Museum of the Great Lakes in Kingston, Ontario. Mr. Bleasby also wrote a long article about Cayuga which was published in *Freshwater - A Journal of Great Lakes Marine History*, 1994.

In 1996 Jim Smith of Niagara-on-the-Lake built a model of Cayuga. This model was on display in Niagara-on-the-Lake and he

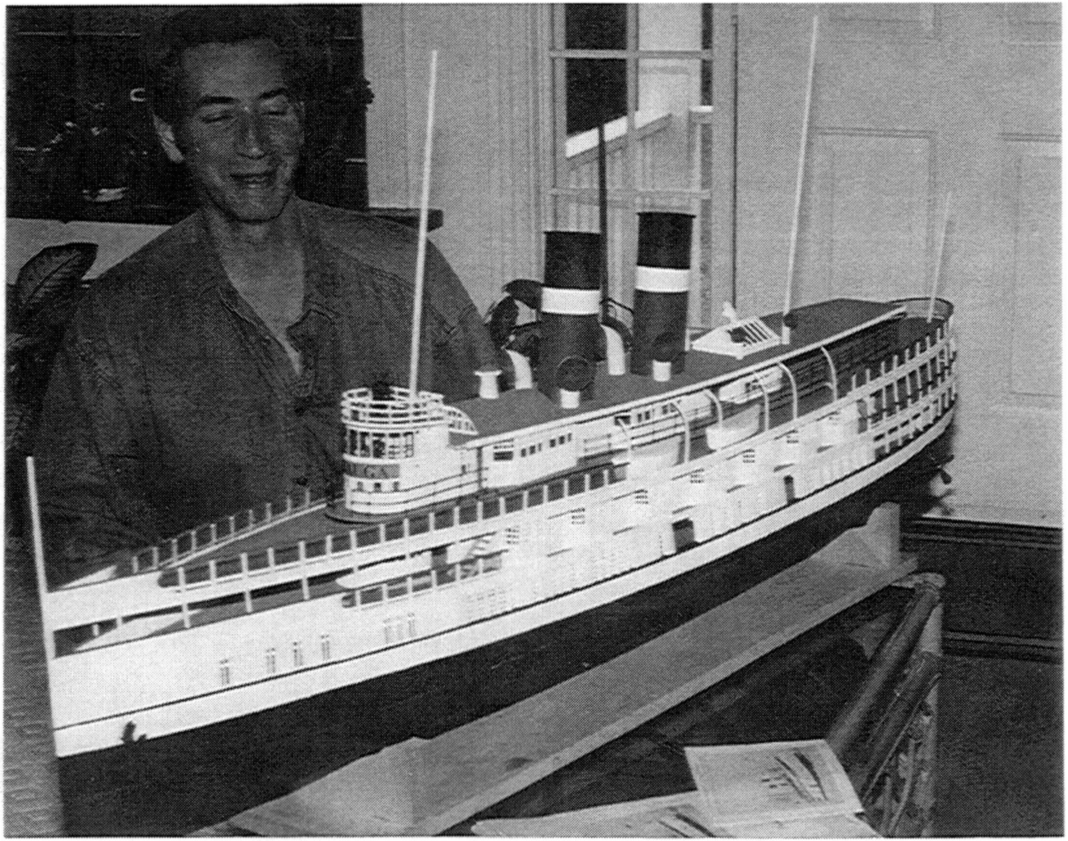

Jim Smith, Niagara-on-the-Lake and the model he built
1996

hopes to find a permanent location for it. Jim's memories of Cayuga are published in *Memories of Cayuga - Ontario's Love Boat*, 1995.

There are still many passengers and crew who remember Cayuga. They own small pieces of her, display photos and paintings in their homes and photo albums. Mention Cayuga and they are pleased to relate their stories. Now there are two books about Cayuga, for thosc who ncvcr sailcd on hcr, to catch a glimpse of Toronto's past and her much loved "ship of romance".

Model detail - built by Jim Smith, Niagara-on-the-Lake

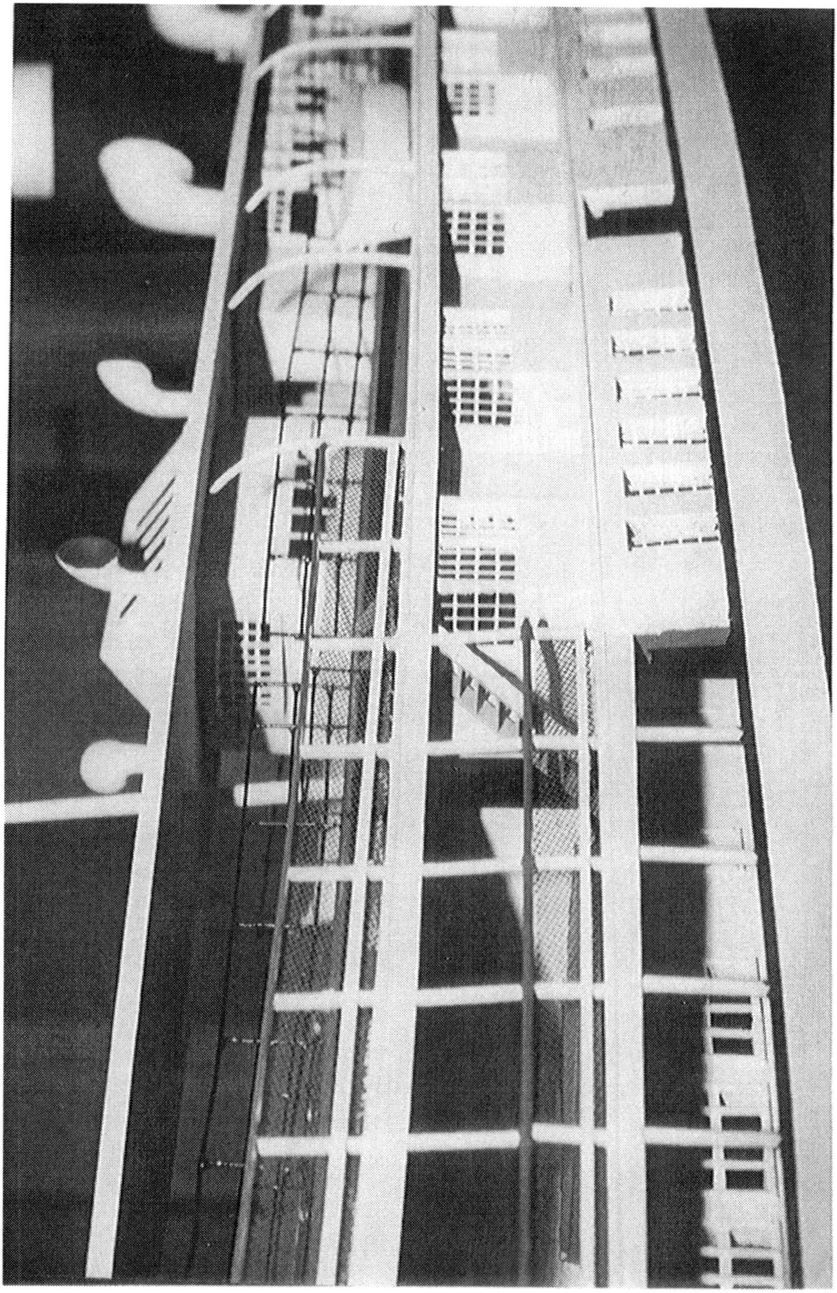

Model detail - built by Jim Smith, Niagara-on-the-Lake

Marine Museum - Toronto - Postcard of Cayuga 's Navigating Island in the Cayuga Room

Author presenting first book on Cayuga to Ian Vincent of the Toronto Historical Society - Oct. 1995

The Owners

NIAGARA NAVIGATION COMPANY

The Niagara Navigation Co. was formed in 1878 for the purpose of servicing the route between Toronto and Niagara. Later this route was extended to include Lewiston.

Other small shipping companies had steamships on Lake Ontario and passengers travelling from one destination to another often had to change ships. Mergers and takeovers resulted to form larger, stronger links.

Niagara Navigation Co. took over the Turbine Steamship Co. One of their ships was the Turbinia. Before merging with the Richelieu and Ontario Navigation Co., Niagara Navigation negotiated a merger with the Hamilton Steamboat Co., founded in 1887.

Niagara Navigation Co., in the early 1900s, became the most successful passenger service on Lake Ontario. There were six sailings per day to Niagara-on-the-Lake and Queenston, and six return sailings.

"It was found very early that the trip up the river is the main attraction to the route..."

Barlow Cumberland

A Century of Sail and Steam on the Niagara River

This was a statement in the report of Niagara Navigation Company's first year of business, 1878. The steamship Chicora, (built in 1864, sank in Toronto harbour in 1919 after colliding with a drifting log during a gale) did not sail on Sunday, only on week days. On Wednesday and Saturday afternoons Chicora sailed to Queenston Heights and later on to Lewiston.

A round-trip fare was $ 1.00 but was gradually reduced. On Wednesday and Saturday afternoon passengers could sail on Chicora for 50¢ return.

The Niagara Navigation Co. was an aggressive company. As they were not connected with the railways, they had to issue their own tickets and provide their own agents. The Toronto to Niagara-on-the-Lake route had heavy competition from ships of other companies. One avenue of business was to offer special packages to societies and churches. In this way they enticed passengers away from thc othcr companics.

Niagara Navigation Co. introduced "An Extension Ticket", an excursion to the Falls. Visitors to Niagara Falls could sail down the river, across the lake to Toronto and return. This was a reduced rate excursion to introduce their company's service. At Lewiston, the company allowed everyone aboard that wanted to come "...whether they had purchased tickets or had tickets from other companies." This developed into a lucrative business.

Docking at Niagara-on-the-Lake was extremely difficult because other ships were already docked. "When coming into the river Chicora had to be driven sharp across from the point at the Fort (Niagara) on the United States side to the dock on the Niagara side...". Coming down river with the current "...it was less dangerous but a more difficult maneuver. The steamers always move swiftly in the quick current which sweeps past Fort George to the docks."

In Toronto Chicora docked at Yonge St.

From here she made two trips a day through the busy western gap. The eastern gap, which Cayuga used, was not built until many years latcr. Somctimcs Chicora had bands playing for the passengers.

From the report of Niagara Navigation Co.'s first year this comment:

> *"Boats often run better on some days than they do on others; it may be the character of the coal, the direction of the wind or the disposition of the firemen...".*

In 1880 Niagara Navigation Co. purchased dock frontage at Lewiston. By 1881 their competitors for the Niagara River route were gone. They now had exclusive control.

In 1881 Chicora began carrying a new group of passengers. On the 5th of June, at Niagara-on-the-Lake, the first camp began for volunteer militia. On the morning run from Toronto, Chicora carried the Toronto Field Battery. This became an annual gathering.

By 1896 Niagara Navigation Co. Had three steamships on the Niagara River route. A third ship, designed by Arendt Angstrom, was the Corona, launched in 1896 at the foot of Bathurst St. In 1893 the steamship Chippewa became Niagara Navigation Co.'s sccond ship.

From Queenston Heights to Niagara Falls passengers travelled by electric railway. This route was along the top of the river bank beside Niagara Gorge. On the American side was a similar electric railway. However, this route was down in the gorge a little above the water's edge.

In 1899 the estate of Duncan Millay sold the Niagara-on-the-Lake docks to the Niagara Navigation Co. Included in this sale was the ship yard of the Niagara Dock Co.

On March 3rd, 1906 steamship Cayuga was launched into Lake Ontario. It was 1907 before she went into service for the company. Cayuga became the company's fourth ship on the Niagara route. In 1895 the Cibola, owned by Niagara Navigation Co., burned at Lewiston dock.

In 1906 "The Lord's Day Act" had a profound impact on passenger service. From 12 o'clock on Saturday afternoon until 12 o'clock on Sunday was the time period stipulated in the Act as a day of rest. This meant that workers had a half day holiday on Saturday which for them began at 1:00 p.m. As well it meant that "...any kind of vessel or boat uscd for convcying passcngcrs or frcight by water..." couldn't sail on Sundays.

In 1911 the Niagara Navigation Co. merged with Richelieu and Ontario Navigation Co. Ltd. Two years later this company was merged into the Canada Steamship Co.

RICHELIEU & ONTARIO NAVIGATION COMPANY

Water transportation was a series of stops from port to port as there were many shipping companies. Each one had its local route and none of them carried passengers from, for example, Montreal, Quebec to Buffalo, New York. Some of the companies mutually agreed to carry passengers from rival companies which erupted into an era of mergers. Richelieu and Ontario had an agreement with Niagara Navigation Co. but in 1912 they bought them out. A year later this company was part of a larger merger which became the Canada Steamship Lines.

With simple beginnings in 1845 La Compagnie du Richelieu began with a steamboat service on the Richelieu River. Two years earlier, 1843, a canal had been completed allowing ships passage from Lake Champlain to the St. Lawrence River. Jacques-Filex Sincennes was a merchant in Sorel who had experience as a pilot, as well as that of purser, on the St. Lawrence. Farmers in the Richelieu Valley had problems transporting their produce to bigger markets. La Compagnic du Richclicu's first boat was a paddle wheel steamer touring barge named the *Richelieu* that stopped at small towns along the Richelieu River. From Sorel, where the St. Lawrence joins the Richelieu River, the steamboat made its way to Montreal carrying the farmers' produce.

Capital for this vcnturc was raiscd by investors, the farmers, local residents and Sincennes. The first meeting of the company was held at St. Charles. This water transportation was an immediate success.

The *Richelieu* made two trips a week. As well as produce the vessel carried passengers. Stopping at Chambly passengers could visit the old fort. On Sunday *Richelieu* stopped at St. Antoine or St. Ours for passengers and crew to attend Mass. When rivals emerged on the same route, a working alliance was agreed on.

As La Compagnie du Richelieu became more successful the investors changed. Prominent financiers replaced the farmers. Although still a major part of the company,

Jacques-Filex Sincennes was now outranked by the Montreal investors. The head office was moved to Montreal and Sincennes moved with it. A ncw compctitor was thc railway.

Declines in profits were a result of the cholera epidemics that discouraged passengers from travelling, as well as from the competition. In 1853 with shipping revenues drastically reduced on the Richelieu River, the company abandoned the route. They decided to compete against other shipping companies on the St. Lawrence River.

To be a vital competitor, La Compagnie du Richelieu needed better ships. They ordered two ships built in Montreal. One was named *Victoria*, after the present Queen, and the second named *Napoleon*. Both ships were built for speed to gain an edge over the competilion. Waler lransportalion became a race.

It was a dangerous time for "stokers" who fed the flames with whatever would make the steam pressure rise. Barrels of resin, or grease, were used to raise the pressure. Captains wanted to win the race for their company. Pulverized colophonium (a resin from turpentine) was sprinkled on coal to make it burn more fiercely and produce greater power. As well, the Captains used aggressive maneuvering. Sometimes the ships were close together with passengers jeering from each ship at who was the fastest. This competition led to disaster.

In 1857, at four o'clock in the afternoon, the ship *Montreal* of the Torrance line, and *Napoleon*, were racing out of Quebec. The *Napoleon* was ahead. Suddenly the *Montreal* caught fire! Passengers and crew tried to put the fire out but all efforts failed. The Captain ordered the ship run aground eight hundred feet from shore. The tide was running swiftly downstream in six and a half feet of water.

Panic ensued. Two lifeboats were lowered - one capsized and the other was overcrowded and sank. *Napoleon* tried to rescue the passengers by backing downstream. A few were saved but 253 people died. This ended the competitive races.

La Compagnie du Richelieu was the best competitor and the Torrance Line was merged with them. Then a strong rival appeared, the Royal Mail Line, which as the name states, carried mail. The two companies came to an agreement to prevent competition and fare reduction. They decided that if one company madc morc profit than thc othcr, thc excess profit would be divided equally. This agreement gave La Compagnie du Richelieu fifteen profitable years.

In 1860 La Compagnie du Richelieu bought smaller shipping lines which added seven ships and two more barges. More ships were ordered in the next seven years and the earnings, year after year, were in excess of its capital. But this could not last forever.

The Canadian Steam Navigation Co. was offered a deal. Hugh Allan, the owner, accepted $4,000.00 for five years for diverting his ships elsewhere, which he accepted. He also invested in La Compagnie du Richelieu and was elected to the Board of Directors. From the inside, Allan pressured them to surrender control to his company.

After Allan sold a good ship to their competitor Union Navigation Co., he made an offer to La Compagnie du Richelieu to merge with his company Canadian Steam Navigation. The offer was rejected. He then sold two more ships to the competition.

There was a merger between the two companies which became Richelieu and Ontario Navigation Co. Unfortunately, in spite of good efforts, the profits fell.

In 1882 Louis-Adelard Senecal seized control of the company. Three years later the company acquired two ferry companies that carried passengers from the Island of Montreal to the south shore of Quebec. The Victoria Bridge connection was only for railway traffic. In 1886 Richelieu and Ontario Navigation Co. purchased the Saguenay Line and now had ships sailing from Saguenay to Toronto - an eight hundred mile route. It was not until after Senecal's death in 1887 that the directors discovered that he was siphoning funds from the company for private use.

Richelieu and Ontario Navigation Co. struggled for seven years until it was finally rescued by a syndicate headed by Louis-Joseph Forget. Passengers who once travelled mainly for business, were now travelling for pleasure.

When Richelieu and Ontario Navigation Co. was back to a profitable service, three luxury paddle wheeled steamboats were ordered. The interiors were ornate and spacious and attracted the tourists. Added to the company were modern hotels that the ships took their passengers to for exquisite holidays. Forgct stccrcd thc company through ten prosperous years. His nephew Joseph-David Rodolphe Forget, in 1905, took over the company after Louis-Joseph retired to other projects. In 1911 rumours erupted about another merger including the Richelieu and Ontario Navigation Co.

In 1912 Richelieu and Ontario merged with the Niagara Navigation Co. as the principal company. This did not stop the rumours of an amalgamation of shipping companies proposed by Grant Morden. Also, British capital was buying large shares in Richelieu and Ontario Navigation.

The board members were in a precarious position by not entering into negotiations for the merger of many smaller shipping companies into an enormous operation. Finally Richelieu and Ontario succumbed in 1913 and the Canada Steamship Co. became the major shipping company with routes from "Liverpool to the Great Lakes."

CANADA STEAMSHIP LINES

In 1911 Walter Grant Morden, inexperienced in business but an expert in negotiating, attended a meeting of the Directors of the Richelieu and Ontario Navigation Co. A young man, dressed in stylish London fashion, he appeared to be a non-entity. However, his goal was to change Ontario's shipping and amalgamate all the small companies.

A persuasive bargainer, he was skilled in getting what he wanted and did not stop until he did! Financial backing came from England rather than from the United States.

Grant Morden used the argument of preventing an American take-over of Canadian waterways, through his merger, to make it successful. Also helping with this merger, as an investor for English capital and his own money, was Lord Furness.

Canada had to get away from its pattern of small shipping companies working against each other. This was the other argument Grant Morden presented to Lord Furness. As well, a Canadian shipping line could connect with that of Lord Furness' thereby ensuring easier travel from Liverpool, England to the American continent.

Passengers travelling for recreation in Canada would want to travel the Great Lakes and the St. Lawrence. Along with this advantage was the future growth of shipping Canadian products such as wheat, coal and iron. The merger would mean nothing without the Richelieu and Ontario Navigation Co.

Northern Navigation Co. was an amalgamation of small companies which began merging in 1880. This company controlled shipping in Georgian Bay connecting with the Grand Trunk Railway.

As the freight carried by the railway grew, so did the number of ships needed to carry it. Built for Northern Navigation was the Huronic and Hamonic. Later the Noronic was built for passengers and freight. Grant Morden realized that the only way to control this company was by a take-over.

Enlisted in 1911 to purchase shares was

James Playfair who was already well known for his shipping concerns on the Great Lakes. Soon he acquired 259 shares of Northern Navigation and publicly announced he would buy more for $ 125.00 a share. Before long he had 90% of the capital stock. Grant Morden had accomplished the first step in his plan. The Richelieu and Ontario Navigation Co. was next but it wasn't as easy as the Northern Navigation Co.

Once again shipping shares were purchased. Rumours circulated that they were being purchased by an influential British investor.

The Directors of Richelieu and Ontario Navigation ignored the talk of a merger. They were the largest navigation company on Canada's inland waterways. Grant Morden used another tool in his quest for amalgamation.

The Directors of the Richelieu and Ontario Navigation Co. allowed Grant Morden's proposal a hearing at their board meeting. Morden suggested they take over the others but with a condition. Grant Morden and associates must be elected to the Board.

It was supposed to be a private session but afterwards Morden gave a story to the press. He stated there would be a ten million dollar mcrgcr of thc Richclicu and Ontario Navigation Co., the Inland Navigation Co. and the Furness Steamship Co.

There was little hope of refusing this offer. Already Richelieu and Ontario Navigation Co. shares had been acquired by Lord Furness. Six weeks after the offer, the merger was approved. However, Grant Morden was not in control of the company.

Only one third of the 15 Board members were Morden's supporters. During the years 1911 - 1913 a power struggle ensued between Board members.

The 10 Directors, who were original Board members, opposed Grant Morden's opinions on how the company should operate. On Feb. 19, 1913 at the Annual Meeting, Morden finally took control.

It was a fierce battle for votes to elect a new Board. A slate of Directors was proposed by Grant Morden against the old Board members. At six o'clock in the evening it was announced that Morden and associates had received the majority of votes.

The President, Sir Rodolphe Forget had been re-elected but he immediately resigned. It had been a hard struggle for Grant Morden but hc now controllcd thc amalgamation of shipping companies.

For a few months the new name of the company was Canada Transportation Lines Limited. In December 1913 the name was changed to the Canada Steamship Lines. One of the steamships in the fleet was S.S. Cayuga.

Although Canada Steamship Lines looked financially healthy, there were problems with the ships it had acquired through the mergers. Many of the ships were old, over-valued and too many stocks had been issued. This did nol slop Granl Morden's quest for companies to add to Canada Steamship Lines.

In 1913 four more shipping companies became part of Canada Steamship Lines. The Ontario and Quebec Navigation Company; the Lake Ontario and Bay of Quinte Steamship Lines; the Canadian Interlake Lines; and the Quebec and Gulf Ports Steamship Company. Canada Steamship Lines now had a huge monopoly on shipping Canada's inland waterways. In 1914 World War I erupted in Europe.

Many of the Canada Steamship Lines ships were refurbished for ocean sailing. These were used to transport regiments to England as well as cargo and munitions. Some of the ships were lost, sixteen sunk in transit.

Grant Morden sought and succeeded in obtaining a military post. He became Personal Staff Officer Overseas to the Minister of Defense.

The financial backing by British sources resulted in two Boards controlling Canada Steamship Lines. One was located in London, England and they had the final say on operational decisions. The other Board was located in Montreal.

In 1914 capital was necessary and the London Board required a .05% commission as well as collateral - the entire assets of Canada Steamship Lines. After the war, in 1919, Joseph Norcross, then President, travelled to London, England, with a new plan for Canada Steamship Lines.

With the loss of so many ships he proposed that Canada Steamship Lines expand the routes. The company entered trans-Atlantic shipping. However it was not a profitable venture. Canada Steamship Lines was too small to bc cfficicnt. By 1920 asscts and ships of the Quebec Steamship Company had to be sold to Furness, Withy and Company for two million dollars.

Joseph Norcross took Canada Steamship Lines further into debt. He had been waiting for the opportunity to purchase the Montreal Transportation Company. The company was purchased for more than three million dollars. More debt was incurred with the purchase of the Davie Shipbuilding and Repairing Company in Quebec.

To get this company into contention for building ships would lake more money thal Canada Steamship Lines didn't have. Grant Morden saw an answer to the money problem. Canada Steamship Lines should merge with a steel company in Nova Scotia. First there would have to be a merger of the steel companies.

After the war the economic situation was not good. The steel industry was in a decline and could not offer needed capital to Canada Steamship Lines. The Directors declined Grant Morden's proposal.

In 1921 Canada Steamship Lines had trouble borrowing more money. And Grant Morden was no longer a member of the Board but he still had a large block of shares. In 1920 he was Deputy Chairman of the London Advisory Committee. Joseph Norcross was forced to seek money from the financiers of New York.

One of the companies acquired by Canada Steamship Lines was the St. Lawrence and Chicago Steam Navigation Company which was generating revenue.

In 1922 William H. Coverdale took on the job of surveying Canada Steamship Lines for financial worth. Later he was appointed President, a position he held for twenty-seven years.

One of the first things in restructuring Canada Steamship Lines was reducing the power of the London Advisory Committee. Grant Morden was ejected from the Committee and finally in 1932 the Committee was disbanded.

In assessing the fleet of Canada Steamship Lines William Coverdale discovered many obsolete, disintegrating ships that were sitting idle at docks. These were sold or scrapped relieving the company of the yearly three million dollar debt to keep them afloat. Thc occan scrvicc was complctcly discontinued in 1927.

After reducing unnecessary debt, in his first five years as President, William Coverdale acquired sixty-one more ships for passengers as well as freight. He also purchased Century Coal Company and merged with the Great Lakes Transportation Company and George Hall Coal and Shipping Corporation. Canada Steamship Lines was returning to financial prosperity. Then in 1929 the Great Depression hit the world.

The company struggled from 1929 until 1937 when nel profils increased marginally. Recovery was almost assured when World War II was declared. Iron ore and coal had to be transported to the steel mills. Ships were also sent to become part of the Atlantic fleets. Five ships were lost, one torpedoed in the St. Lawrence River.

The Davie shipyard began building merchant vessels ordered by the Government of Canada. Canada Steamship Lines was financially sound.

Submitted by Jim Smith from Don Van Alstine

William Coverdale, in 1944, decided that passenger ships were top priority. New ships must be built costing four million dollars. After the war passengers no longer preferred steamship travel. Steamship Cayuga, a ship that carried soldiers from Toronto to Niagara-on-the-Lake for training, was nearing the end of her phase as part of the Canada Steamship Lines' "Great White Fleet".

Before the wars the era was one of enticing passengers to "take to" the luxury of leisurely water travel. Scenic travel along the St. Lawrence River gave passengers breath-taking views. Crossing Lake Ontario was a romantic two hour sail, sometimes with bands playing on moonlight cruises. Spotless ships provided elegant adventures to everyone regardless of social status. Shooting the rapids was an incomparable thrill. During the summer months Canada Steamship Lines was Canada's largest employer.

Most of the summer employees were students. They worked as waiters and waitresses; soda fountain dispensers, busboys, porters, cabin boys, ticket sellers, messboys, to name a few of the many jobs. On

September 17, 1949 the fire that destroyed Noronic destroyed what was left of the passenger service of the Canada Steamship Lincs.

The Government of Canada was urged to introduce and enforce tough safety requirements. Cayuga was fitted with fire detectors, alarm sirens, a public address system on all decks at a high cost. Every thirty minutes 24 hours a day, a Fire Patrol checked each deck. Installed were fireproof bulkheads, a sprinkler system and a steam smothering apparatus in the boiler, lamp and paint rooms.

In 1950 the only ships remaining of the "Great White Fleet" were *Cayuga* on Lake Ontario, and on the route from Montreal to Saguenay were the *St. Lawrence*, the *Tadoussac* and the *Richelieu*. The automobile was emerging as the preferred way to travel. Another threat to passenger service was the take-over of Canada Steamship Lines by steel magnate Sir James Dunn.

Canada Steamship Lines was no longer a good investment. The new President was Rodgie McLagan. He wanted freight carriers, not passenger service. During 1952 and 1953

Cayuga sat in dock at Toronto.

In 1953 the citizens of Toronto and area rallied to save their beloved Cayuga. Canada Steamship Lines sold their once profitable passenger ship to a newly formed company, Cayuga Steamship Company Limited.

Cayuga in Toronto Bay 1915 - National Archives of Canada
PA61356 - John Boyd

CAYUGA STEAMSHIP COMPANY

In 1952 Cayuga sat idle at Toronto dock. Canada Steamship Lines could no longer afford the cost of running her or repairs and upgrades. Two years, 1952 - 1953, Cayuga waited in dock to resume cruising across Lake Ontario, filled with excited passengers.

During that time the population became enchanted with cars which allowed for a personal schedule rather than a sailing schedule. But Cayuga would get one last chance to sail on Lake Ontario.

Alan Howard, Roland Michener, Allan Grossman, William M. Wismer and Arthur C.J. Franklin would not let Cayuga be forgotten. In 1953 they formed the Cayuga Steamship Company. First they surveyed the condition of Cayuga. This survey was performed in 1953 by John Stephen, a Marine Surveyor.

Canada Steamship Lines granted them an option to purchase Cayuga for $ 100,000.

Submitted by Jim Smith from Don Van Alstine

Along with the purchase of Cayuga came a parcel of land, the Niagara Harbour at Niagara-on-the-Lake. At Queenston, docking privileges were included.

In Niagara-on-the-Lake the property extended 800 feet back from the river and included an enclosed yacht basin that generated revenue from mooring rentals. The dock had a wooden passenger shelter, roofed for inclement weather or shade for waiting passengers. At Queenston there was a steel and concrete dock with various shelters and a ticket office.

The potential for passengers, so said the Prospectus of 1953, was enormous. The company estimated passengers would come from Toronto with a population of 1,160,000 people. Buffalo residents would travel on Cayuga as well as residents from Niagara Falls, (Canada and New York), St. Catharines and communities along the river. The potential passenger estimate was 2,700,000. Then there were tourists to the Niagara region estimated at 2,000,000. Cayuga could be a prosperous operation for investors.

Another area of passengers was from the Niagara Military Camp. The Camp had been re-opened in 1952 and troops from Toronto, with equipment, could easily travel across Lake Ontario on the Cayuga. Friends and rclativcs wcrc surc to follow, on this samc route, to visit the camp. Passengers may also want to travel to view the Sir Adam Beck hydro project at Niagara Falls.

Cayuga Steamship Company had to raise, from the shares sold, a minimum of $140,000.00. This amount would cover the purchase price as well as outfitting and operating Cayuga for the 1954 season. Alan Howard, the Managing Director, would receive a salary of $ 5,000.00 a year from the operating funds. He would be the only director to receive payment for services.

During lhe firsl year of operalion Cayuga Steamship Company, and its subsidiary Cayuga Navigation Company, lost $ 10,000.00. Salaries for the 75 crew totaled $ 87,000.00 plus another $ 10,000.00 to feed them. Fuel oil totaled almost $ 55,000.00 and other expenses made a grand total of $205,000.00.

Passenger, freight and other revenue totaled almost $ 250,000.00. There was a bank loan of $ 30,000.00 to repay with interest. Other staff salaries totaled $28,000.00.

The shares sold totaled 41,132 ranging in price from $ 5.00 per share to $ 7.00. Of these shares, 800 had been given for services rendered.

The Directors' Report by Roland Michener, from the second Annual Meeting held on Feb. 21, 1955, gave further details. The report stated that the weather during the summer of 1954 was unfavourable for travel in the months of June and August. In spite of this 194,778 passengers, estimated on one way fares, was an increase over 1951, the last year of service, of 40,000 passengers. Cayuga made 436 single trips from Toronto to Queenston, including stops at Niagara-on-the-Lake.

In July 1954 a good profit was made as well as in August and September. With a two year lay-up there had been insufficient advance promotion and bookings which hindered better profits. To alleviate this in the 1955 season, fares would be increased slightly with a revised sailing schedule - and the hope of good weather. In June 1954 the estimated loss was $ 28,000.00 and the actual cash loss

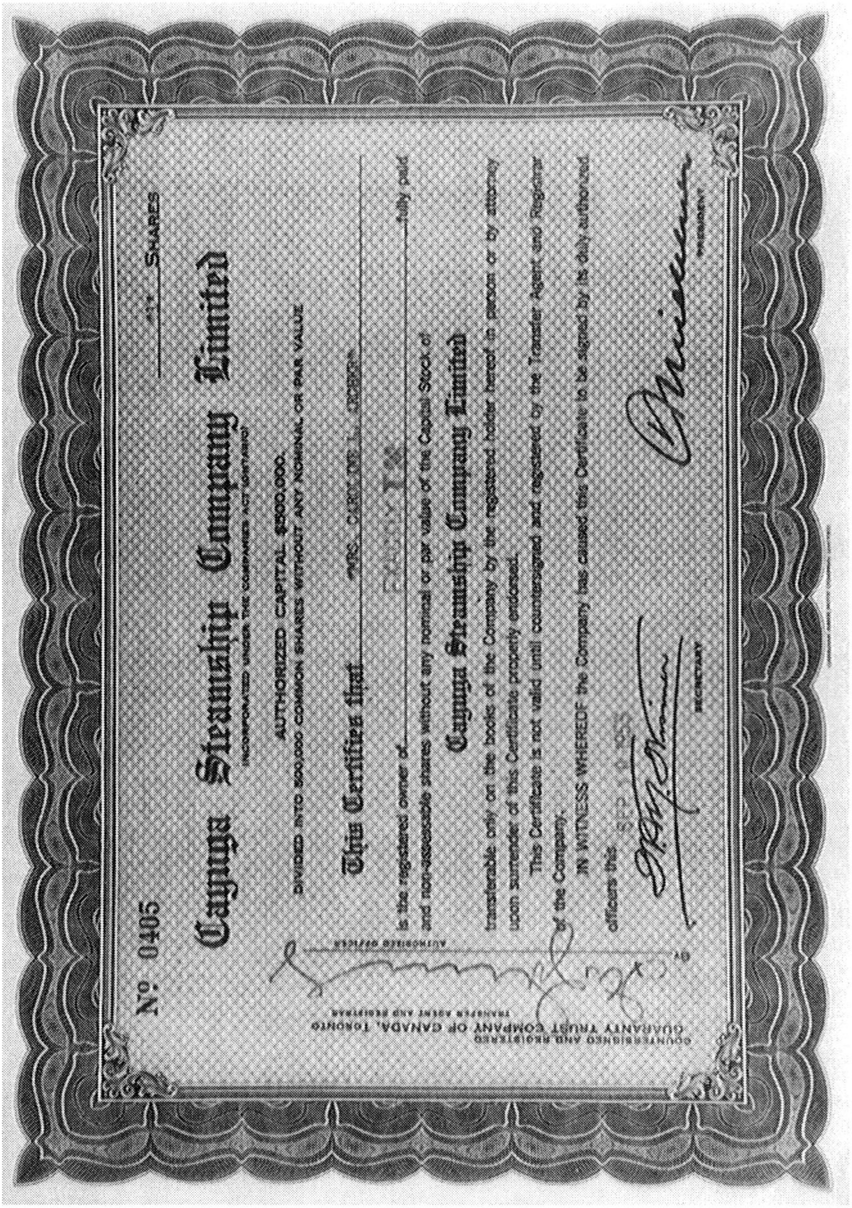

Stock Certificate from the Cayuga Steamship Co.
Toronto Historical Board - # 1991.10.1

by September was $ 4,740.07.

The 1955 season for Cayuga was even less profitable. Only 193,375 passengers travclled on Cayuga in spitc of hot summer weather. Winter weather also caused a profit drain. The dock at Niagara-on-the-Lake was destroyed and there was also damage to the Queenston dock from an unusually severe ice jam on the Niagara River.

In the Directors' Report for 1955 Roland Michener and the Board made suggestions for increased revenue. There should be more promotion, advance bookings of excursions and parties, with employment of full time promotion staff and public relations advisors.

Another suggestion was an increase of fares, replace the live orchestra, who entertained the dancers on moonlight cruises, with recorded music. An incentive to travel on Cayuga would be a licensed bar as well as more entertainment and prizes.

The last suggestion would be to discontinue the service and sell Cayuga. She would sail one more season during the summer of 1956.

Once again Cayuga did not make a

Eastern Gap Light House Keeper Alf Winslow
Globe & Mail - June 4, 1954 - # 54154-3
In 1908 Alf Winslow sold popcorn on Cayuga

Pipers celebrate Cayuga's return to service
Globe & Mail - June 4, 1954 - # 54156-1

Mayor Alan Lamport lets off steam and blows the whistle
Globe & Mail - June 4, 1954

Cayuga passengers - June 4, 1954
Globe & Mail - # 54154-4

300 people cruise on Cayuga - Globe & Mail
June 4, 1954 - # 54154-1

profit, incurring further losses. Only 135,527 passengers travelled on her, possibly due to the cold summer weather. The promotional programmc had bccn bcttcr but could not counter act the poor weather. There had been two special all-day cruises, a pre-season one from Coburg to Rochester and another from Toronto to Queenston Heights. Unfortunately, it had not generated the anticipated passenger traffic. Cayuga Steamship Company needed at least $75,000.00 to continue operating Cayuga.

On Jan. 29, 1957 the Annual Meeting was held. Two hundred shareholders attended to discuss Cayuga's fate. The shareholders approved the application for a liquor license but it would not be determined by the Liquor Control Board until June. This was too late to re-fit Cayuga for the summer season. Also agreed by the shareholders was the proposal to issue debentures to give security to unpaid creditors, and raise money to pay off these creditors. Cayuga Steamship Company was $ 50,000.00 in debt.

Consideration was given to selling some of the assets, including Cayuga for scrap. Or the company could sell the docks and land,

Submitted by Jim Smith from Don Van Alstine

keeping Cayuga intact for use in inland waterways elsewhere in the world. Because Cayuga was too long to navigate through the present locks on the St. Lawrence River, the company couldn't move her until the St. Lawrence Seaway was completed. The shareholders preferred to find some way to continue operating Cayuga.

Cayuga Steamship Company called for tenders in the sale of surplus land at Niagara-on-the-Lake, but would retain their docking facilities. Already they had received inquiries about this purchase and were hopeful that they would secure a good price. Shareholders were given the opportunity to purchase secured debentures at $ 100.00 each, Series B, for 100 shares of capital stock. This ensured one final season for Cayuga during the summer of 1957.

The land and buildings at Niagara-on-the-Lake were sold for $ 42,000.00. Some of the creditors were paid but Cayuga Steamship Company needed credit to operate Cayuga. Shareholders subscribed to the amount of $16,500.00 but Cayuga Steamship Company needed another $ 25,000.00. Further debentures were offered until Sept. 3, 1957.

Cpt. J.D. Strachan - Globe & Mail
June 4, 1954 - # 54154-2

At the beginning of the season Capt. J.D. Strachan suffered a heart attack. More losses were incurred totaling $ 70,000.00. Cayuga could not continue under these circumstances and made her last trip on Sept. 3, 1957. A valiant effort had been made by the Board and shareholders to keep Cayuga, a well loved ship, sailing.

Once again Cayuga was confined to a dock in Toronto, never again to carry passengers across Lake Ontario.

New owners in 1960, Charles Santos and Joe McCarthy had plans for Cayuga. They wanted to re-fit her as a floating restaurant. However in 1961 Greenspoon Bros. a wrecking company, bought Cayuga and in late July began dismantling her.

An era of pleasure cruising ended with the loss of Cayuga. Cars carried passengers along the Queensway and over the toll bridge near Hamilton. Many years later a small boat cruised Lake Ontario under the name of Cayuga II. It lasted one season and because of its size could not offer the pleasure of strolling the decks or chasing seagulls like the original Cayuga. Thirty-five years later passengers and crew still remember fondly the

Submitted by Jim Smith from Don Van Alstine

Humiliating end for Cayuga at Toronto
Marine Museum, Kingston, Ont. # 980-148-1

delights of sailing and dancing on Cayuga. I am glad that I was one of the passengers for 12 years near the end of her era. Farewell to a grand lady of the lake.

Alan Howard, seated, Curator W.J. Smith, Toronto Historical Bd.
receives wheel house equipment from Wm. Greenspoon
Globe & Mail - Aug. 4, 1961 - Harry McLorinan

ALAN N. HOWARD
1914 - 1986

The Cayuga Steamship Company Prospectus lists Alan Howard as a Public Relations Counsel as well as the Treasurer and Managing Director. These are only part of who Alan was.

In 1918, when Alan was four years old, his family moved to Centre Island in Toronto. He lived on the island until 1960 when the family home was demolished to enlarge the public park. When the future of the remaining island homes was under discussion by city politicians, Alan joined the fight. The residents fought for thirty years to preserve the homes as permanent residences.

Preservation of Toronto's history was one of Alan's ambitions. Ships were his greatest interest. With his artistic talent he painted lake vessels, famous ocean liners, historic buildings, especially in England where his family emigrated from.

Using his natural talent for public

Sentiment couldn't save her - Globe & Mail
Aug. 10, 1961

speaking, Alan held his audience spell bound at his lectures. Most often his lectures were given without using notes.

Several organizations welcomed Alan as curator. In Feb. 1961 Alan became the first Curator of the Marine Museum of Upper Canada located in the Stanley Barracks at what was then called Toronto's Exhibition Park (now called Toronto's Exhibition Place). Twenty years later, Feb. 1981, he retired. A special "Soiree" was held in his honour attended by important personages such as the Mayor of Toronto, Art Eggleton, and Lieutenant-Governor, the Hon. John Black Aird.

Alan was one of the founding members of the Toronto Marine Historical Society as well as an honourary member. In later years he became a member of the Executive Committee.

K.R. MacPherson, in his article in Scanner Magazine, 1986, says:

> *"Alan Howard, a man of many interests, did not have an easy life. Every movement and every activity posed a special problem for him, but Alan faced and*

> *surmounted these difficulties with a courage and determination that few of us could ever muster."*

Mr. Greenspoon of Greenspoon Bros., who dismantled Cayuga, joked about the pieces of Cayuga that Alan wanted. He said that hc fclt hc should ask Alan what parts of Cayuga Greenspoon Bros. could have.

In an article written by Don Evans, *The Saga of Toronto's Best Loved Ship, S.S. Cayuga..."* he mentions that Alan often remarked "On a June morning at five minutes to nine, I hear a warning whistle, one short blast, the gang-plank taken away, followed by another short whistle for 'let go aft'. The Captain rings for 'slow ahead' on the port engine and the Cayuga slides off. The telegraph rings "Astern' and as the ship starts backing the remaining forward cable is cast off. Then I hear throbbing engines, a prolonged warning blast as Cayuga backs out from the Yonge St. slip. She turns in the bay and once again heads south-east for the Eastern Gap, Lake Ontario and the Niagara River ports."

Cayuga Captains

Mate at the wheel - submitted by Jim Smith from Don Van Alstine

CAYUGA CAPTAINS

Candidates for First Mates and Masters' Certificates are required to have an elementary knowledge of theoretical plane trigonometry and to be able to solve problems in plane and right-angled spherical trigonometry.

Nicholls concise Guide
for Mates and Masters to the
Local Marine Board
Examine 1926

Second Mates need to know:

- *knowledge of principals*
- *practical navigation*
- *chart work*
- *cargo work and ship construction*

First Mates need to know:

- *practical navigation*
- *chart work*
- *cargo work and ship construction*
- *meteorology*
- *ship stability*

Masters need to know:

- *practical navigation*
- *meteorology*
- *ship construction and stability*
- *compass*
- *ship's business*
- *engineering*

"Self Examination for Masters and Mates" - Brown, Son & Ferguson Glasgow

* * * * *

For three years Commodore John McGiffen was Cayuga's senior captain when she was owned by the Richelieu and Ontario Navigation Company. Commodore McGiffen also served on the Chippewa, Chicora, Cibola and Corona. In 1903 Captain McGiffen earned his title of Commodore because of his carefulness and good judgement.

As captain of the Chippewa he left Toronto at 7:00 a.m. during heavy gale conditions on an extremely choppy lake. Five miles out from the south shore of Lake Ontario a heavy fog shrouded the coast line. Off Niagara at the Bell Buoy, Capt. McGiffen could not see to enter the river. Rather than risk damage to the Chippewa, he stayed close to the buoy. Remaining there all day, and into the evening, he kept the passengers well fed. Sixteen hours after leaving Toronto, at 11:50 p.m. when Capt. McGiffen could see the land lights, Chippewa docked at Niagara-on-the-Lake. For this concern for ship and passengers, Capt. McGiffen earned the title of Commodore.

Commodore McGiffen suffered from diabetes. He was on duty on Cayuga until several days before his death. In 1910 at the age of 68, he died. In tribute to his excellence the Niagara steamboats lowered their flags to half mast.

In the 1923 listing of captains *Green's Marine Directory* lists Capt. C.H. Mohr on

Captain Charles J. Smith on the bridge of SS Cayuga
from the collection of Toronto Historical Board
Toronto, Ontario - # 1974.61.100

Captain Harry W. Webster on the bridge of SS Cayuga
from the collection of Toronto Historical Board
Toronto, Ontario - # 1974.61.119

Cayuga. However in 1910 Capt. C.J. Smith, who in 1914 became Commodore Smith, was on Cayuga for 21 years. In 1935 two captains shared the duty on Cayuga for almost 20 years.

One was Capt. H.W. Webster. The other was Capt. J.D. Strachan.

James Don Strachan was born in 1888 in the fishing village of Inverallochy, Scotland. It was a rugged village of stone cottages and today, his relatives still live there. At 19 he went to sea on his first ship as a cook. He had never cooked before. One time, while docked somewhere in Australia, he woke up to find a sailor covered in blood trying to get into his bunk. Apparently the drunken sailor had been in a fight and crawled onto the wrong ship.

In 1909 six foot James Strachan married Maggie Gordon whose brother Donald Gordon was known as "The Great Scot". In 1920 he, his wife and family moved to Canada.

They moved to the city of Toronto at Parliament St. and Carlton St. He lived here with his family until 1953, when he and Maggie moved to Scarborough to live with their daughter Isobel.

James Strachan worked on several of the steamships owned by the Canada Steamship Lines. He served on the *Chippewa,* the *Kingston*, then as First Mate on *Cayuga* with Capt. Wcbstcr and scrvcd with him from approximately 1935 to 1954. When Capt. Webster retired James Strachan took over as the captain of *Cayuga* under the ownership of the Cayuga Steamship Company.

Capt. Strachan's daughter Isobel rcmcmbcrs Capt. Wcbstcr. Whcn shc was a child, a couple of times a week, Capt. Webster gave her oranges.

As a child Isobel often sailed on Cayuga with her father in the pilot house but he never allowed her to touch the big wheel. She remembers one time when Cayuga's bow was lifted by high waves. Travelling at that time with three of her friends, she says that they were all sea sick but not her! In rough weather the crew tied down the deck chairs so they wouldn't go overboard into the lake.

When Capt. Strachan, who rolled his own cigarettes, retired, the students bought him a lighter. "We'll have better jobs," was

Cpt. J.D. Strachan - submitted by his daughter Isobel Cooney their comment, "but we'll never have a better boss."

Capt. Strachan lived on *Cayuga* in the summer and his family often came to visit in his two rooms, a bedroom and a sitting room. He could always tell the weather just by looking up at the sky. In the early years he wore a uniform of a navy jacket and white trousers. The later uniform was totally navy. His stiff shirt collars were always starched at the Chinese laundry.

Although he was a calm, unflappable person, he could give the crew a good "dressing down" with his expressive eyes. Capt. Strachan never used swear words and strongly objected to anyone else swearing in his presence.

His daughter Isobel says that one time the men painting Cayuga's interior were swearing while working. Capt. Strachan objected and told them to go outside if they wanted to swear.

Capt. Strachan survived three heart attacks. In approximately 1951, at the age of 63, he suffered one while docking Cayuga. However he thought it was just his bad stomach acting up and took a bit of baking

Cpt. J.D. Strachan - submitted by his daughter
Isobel Strachan

soda. He climbed the ladder to the bridge, which was where Cayuga was steered from during good weather, and brought her into dock at Toronto. By this timc hc was worsc and a doctor was called. Capt. Strachan was given morphine at the hospital. He refused to go home in an ambulance and instead took a taxi. Arriving home, he walked up three flights of stairs and was promptly returned to the hospital.

During the off season Capt. Strachan did many odd jobs. Jobs were hard to find especially during the Great Depression. Capt. Strachan washed cars, was a watchman and helped with painting the deck chairs as well as painting Cayuga.

In 1973, at the age of 85, Capt. Strachan suffered his fourth and fatal heart attack.

In 1941 a certificate of discharge for Mr. C. Santagato lists the master as B. Bongarde. Then in 1957 the relieving master is listed as Capt. D.W. Livingstone.

Information

<u>DESIGNERS</u> - Arendt Angstrom
- L.E. Tornroos

When the idea of building a new steamship was proposed by the Niagara Navigation Co. they wanted the best marine engineer to design it. In 1904 Arendt Angstrom of the Canadian Shipbuilding Co., located at 71 Crescent Rd., in Toronto, had designed many ships that sailed on Lake Ontario. He was born in Sweden and had been Manager of the Bertram Iron Works. He designed ships for the Richelieu & Ontario Navigation Co., the steamers *Montreal, Kingston, Toronto* and *Rapids King.* His design of Cayuga is said to be "one of the most graceful and well proportioned...ever built in Canada."

Edgar Allan Collard - Passage to the Sea

Arendt Angstrom was also a director of the Hamilton Steamboat Co. and a member of the Canadian Association of Naval Architecture which was located in Toronto.

NIAGARA NAVIGATION COMPANY STEAMSHIPS

1878	Chicora - paddle steamer built in 1864 sank in Toronto Harbour 1914
1888	Cibola - paddle steamer burned at Lewiston 1895
1893	Chippewa - paddle steamer 1939 was scrapped
1896	Corona - paddle steamer 1937 was scrapped
1906	Cayuga - propeller driven 1961 was scrapped by Greenspoon Bros.

LAKE ONTARIO

(smallest of the Great Lakes)

The Niagara River is the main source of the 193 mile long lake (311 km). Other rivers feeding it are the Genesee, Oswego, Black River from the south and Trent river from the north. Its greatest width is 53 miles (85 km) and is 245 feet (75 m) above sea level. Its depth is 283 feet (86 m) and at the deepest point is 802 feet (244 m). There is a general surface current that flows east 8 miles a day. The current is strongest along the south shore in the Niagara area.

Lake Ontario stretches from Hamilton, east to Kingston where it flows into the St. Lawrence Seaway. At the Niagara River the south side is American territory and the north side is Canadian.

ANOTHER CAYUGA

In 1895 the Lake Michigan and Lake Superior Transport Company owned a steamship named *Cayuga.* This *Cayuga* collided with a steamer named *Joseph L. Hurd.* On May 10, 1895 Cayuga sank into Lake Michigan with the bow of steamship *Hurd* still embedded in her hull. Efforts were made to raise *Cayuga* from a depth of 106 feet but she remains in Lake Michigan.

from: *Island Seas, Quarterly Journal of the Great Lakes Historical Society Winter 1961*

Reprinted from: *Ships and Shipwrecks in Door County, Wisconsin Volume One, 1961*

BIBLIOGRAPHY

A Century of Steam and Sail on the Niagara River
Barlow Cumberland - 1913
Niagara Navigation Co.
The First Season

Articles by: Francis Petrie
Don Glynn

Britannica CD Rom - 1995

Canada, Past, Present and Future
W.H. Smith - 1852

Cayuga Steamship Company
Prospectus - May 1953
Amendment to Prospectus - May 1953
Prospectus - June 1953
Amendment to Prospectus - June 1953
Condition Survey - May 1953
Annual Report - Oct. 1954
Annual Report - Oct. 1955
Annual Report - Oct. 1956
Report on the Annual Meeting
held on Jan. 29, 1957
Report to Shareholders - Aug. 15, 1957

Fresh Water Vol 9 Number 2 1994
S.S. Cayuga and the Toronto-
Queenston steamer service
J.R.G. Bleasby

Great Lakes Ships We Remember
Editor - Rev. Peter J. Vander Linden
Freshwater Press Inc., Cleveland, Ohio

Green's Marine Directory - 1923

History of Shipbuilding and Naval
Architecture
Garth Wilson

Island Seas Quarterly Journal - 1961

Passage to the Sea - The Story of Canada Steamship Lines
Edgar Allan Collard

Scanner Magazine
Ship of the Month No. 146 - Cayuga
May 1986
Another Crossing in Cayuga - 1986
More About Cayuga, Turbinia and Modjeska - 1986
Alan N. Howard by K.R. MacPherson
Feb. 1986

The Evening Telegram - March 3, 1906

The Globe and Mail - Aug. 10, 1961
- Aug. 14, 1961

The Railway and Shipping World - June 1905

The Saga of Toronto's Best Loved Ship, S.S. Cayuga and her sister ships of the Niagara Navigational Co. - 1994
Don Evans

Toronto Historical Board
S.S. Cayuga 1907 - 1961

Toronto Sun
The Way We Were
Mike Filey

ABOUT THE AUTHOR:

Writing comes easy to Carole. However, it was not until her adult years that she discovered that what she wrote, other people liked to read. Her first published work was a letter to the editor. Since then she has filled filing cabinets and other empty shelf space with stories and articles, many of them published. Her first book was published in 1994, "Journey Into Christmas" and in 1995 "Memories of Cayuga - Ontario's Love Boat".

This year Carole has published the first of her children's stories "The Adventures of Inch Worm Willie".

Now that the Cayuga books are finished, Carole will start publishing her fiction novels.

Carole lives in Scarborough with her husband Gord, daughter Lori, two dogs, Lucky Lady and Sheba, and one cat, Mr. Tommie Blue Socks.